The Internet and Email

Don McLeese

Rourke
Publishing LLC
Vero Beach, Florida 32964

www.rourkepublishing.com

PHOTO CREDITS: © Brasil2: Title Page; © ronfromyork: page 4; © Christopher Meder: page 5, 19; © digitalskillet: page 6 top; © licensed under the terms of the cc-by-sa-2.0dylanparker: page 6 bottom; © Matt Trommer: page 8 top; © Pedro Nogueira: page 10; © Brett Hillyard: page 11; © muellek: page 12; © letty: page 13; © Norman Chan: page 14; © Apple: page 15; © Ioana Drutu: page 17; © Yahoo: page 18 top; © Clement Seveillac: page 20; © Dan Tero: page 21; © Tom England: page 23; © Terry Heaey: page 25; © Stanford: page 26 left, 27 bottom; © Steve Geer: page 27 top; © sweetym: page 28; © compucow: page 31; © coolcaesar: page 32; © aol: page 33; © MWProductions: page 34;© Facebook: page 35; ©Mika/photobank/kiev.ua: page 36;© Rich Legg: page 38; © Mark hatfield": 3; © Zlatko Guzmik: pagw 40; © Symantec: page 41; © ronon: page 43

Editor: Nancy Harris

Cover Design by Nicky Stratford, bdpublishing.com

Interior Design by Renee Brady

Library of Congress Cataloging-in-Publication Data

McLeese, Don.
   The Internet and E-mail / Donald McLeese.
      p. cm. -- (Let's explore technology communications)
   Includes index.
   ISBN 978-1-60472-331-1
   1. Internet--Juvenile literature. 2. Electronic mail systems--Juvenile literature. I. Title.
   TK5105.875.I57M3835 2009
   004.692--dc22
                                        2008019777

Printed in the USA

CG/CG

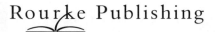

Rourke Publishing

www.rourkepublishing.com – rourke@rourkepublishing.com
Post Office Box 3328. Vero Beach. FL 32964

Contents

CHAPTER ONE

What Is the Internet?

You won't find the Internet on any map. You can't touch it. You can't see it, except on a computer. When you turn off the computer, the Internet disappears. Or does it?

Have you ever thought about how much information is on the Internet? On any given day there are approximately 100 million active Internet domains. If you went to 5,000 different domains every day, it would take you 50 years to look at that many domains. Not to discourage you, but it would be impossible to do this because every day new domains are added while other domains are deleted.

The Internet exists in a place that some people call cyberspace. This is a term invented by a writer named William Gibson and it refers to the electronic world of computer networks, where computers communicate or talk with each other.

The Internet is always there in cyberspace, ready for us to connect with it when we turn on our computers. The Internet is where we send emails, find information that helps us with our homework, or play games.

William Gibson

William Gibson published a novel in 1984 titled *Neuromancer*. This book contains the first mention of the term cyberspace, a word he made up. Gibson has been called a writer of science fiction, telling stories about how science has changed our lives and could change the future.

Do You Know What These Terms Mean?

Term	What Does It Mean?	Additional Information
blog	A blog is a Web log, or journal entry, that a person posts on a Web page.	Blogs are places where people share their thoughts and opinions. Just because you find something on a blog doesn't mean it's accurate.
handle	A handle is your screen name for online chatting.	Since anyone can create a handle and chat online, it's best to chat with friends you know and not strangers.
netiquette	Netiquette is etiquette, or manners, for the Internet.	As with the phone, it is important to use good manners when you send emails or are part of online chats.
spam	Spam is junk email and junk postings on message boards.	Sending spam is very poor netiquette.
spoofing	Spoofing refers to faking, or hiding, your identity on the Internet.	Spoofing is deceptive and is very poor netiquette.
wiki	Wikis are websites where users can update information.	Wikipedia is an example of a wiki. If you are doing research, you should always verify information you get from a wiki with other resources.

CHAPTER TWO

Surfing the Net

Usually, the Internet is simply called the *net*. Most of the places that we visit on the Internet are part of the World Wide Web (www).

The web, as it is often called, consists of so many websites that we can't count them. Schools, stores, newspapers, and magazines have their own websites.

Local governments have websites. Even some families and individuals have their own websites.

Each of these websites has an address, like www.yourname.com. The www stands for World Wide Web. A web address, or domain name, is called an URL. This stands for Uniform Resource Locator. You use the address to locate the website you want to visit.

Fun Fact-Filled Websites:

www.yucky.com
www.funbrain.com
www.brainpop.com

We call visiting a number of different websites surfing the net. This term originally referred to riding the waves of an ocean on a surfboard. While surfing is still a popular sport, the term has a new meaning made popular by Internet users.

You can think of the web as a great big ocean of information, and each website as a wave that you can surf, or read. Keep in mind that there is a big difference between surfing waves and surfing the web. When you're surfing waves, your ride will end. But when you're surfing the web, you can surf from one site to another indefinitely.

Did you know...

In England, the average person spends more time online each day than watching television.

- Time spent online: 164 minutes per day
- Time spent watching television: 148 minutes per day

CHAPTER THREE
Making the Connection

In order to connect to the net, you must have an account with an Internet Service Provider (ISP). Many different kinds of companies provide Internet service. You may get this through your telephone company or your cable TV company. You might receive it through an Internet company such as AOL (America Online). You pay each month for Internet service just as you do for telephone service.

When choosing an ISP it is important to know the download and upload speeds of the different ISPs you are choosing from. Download speed is how fast an ISP can transfer files, such as photos and games, from the Internet to your computer. Upload speed is just the reverse. It is how fast an ISP can transfer files from your computer over the Internet to someone else. Both download and upload speeds are measured in kilobits per second (kb/s).

ISPs with a slow speed are usually cheap. The downside is, you might find it frustrating to play Internet games or do research for homework. While everyone wants a very fast ISP, they often cost more and the extra cost may not be in your parent's budget!

What Countries Have the Fastest Download Speeds?

1. Japan   14,896 kb/s
2. Sweden   8,886 kb/s
3. Latvia   7,714 kb/s
4. Bulgaria   7,106 kb/s
5. Republic of Korea   6,878 kb/s

To find out the download and upload speeds of your current ISP, checkout one of the free websites, such as www.speedtest.net .

A computer also requires other things to connect to the Internet. It needs a modem to make the connection, which can be either inside or outside your computer. It needs a web browser, which allows you to find websites once you have connected to the Internet. You open the browser through a picture, called an icon, on your computer screen. You use the mouse attached to your computer to point at the icon and click twice to open it. (Or you can use a wireless mouse that doesn't need to be attached.) On several laptop computers, you can click on a pad that is part of the computer instead of using a mouse.

An external modem connects to both your computer and your phone line.

Some popular web browsers include Internet Explorer, Netscape, and Safari. Most computers come with one of these already installed or loaded, so that the icon will already be on the screen.

Microsoft and Internet Explorer

Microsoft is the biggest company that develops computer programs. Almost all computers that come with Microsoft programs have Internet Explorer as their browser. Most Apple computers come with Safari as their browser.

CHAPTER FOUR

Search Engines

What if you know what you're looking for on the web, but you do not have a website address?

You can go to a website called a search engine, type in whatever you're looking for and hit search.

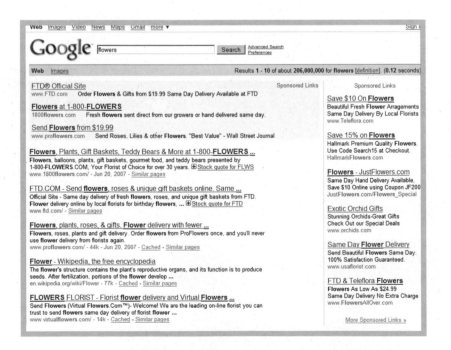

If you were writing a book like this one, you could type in Internet or History of the Internet or World Wide Web. The search engine would give you choices of hundreds, thousands, or even millions of websites you can surf to locate what you're looking for.

It only takes a few seconds for the search engine to do this. Popular search engines include Google (www.google.com) and Yahoo (www.yahoo.com).

Google

In recent years, Google has become such a popular search engine that a lot of people say *google* instead of search. It is now an entry in English language dictionaries. When you need to search for something, you might say, "I'll google that."

Tips for Finding Information Using a Search Engine

- Be specific – if you are writing a state report on Florida and want information on theme parks in Florida, try Florida theme parks instead of just Florida.

- Capitalization doesn't matter – if you are searching for information on Barak Obama, you will get the same results with Barak Obama or barak obama or bArAk obAMA.

- Spelling of words does not have to be perfect – if you are unsure of how a word is spelled, type in your best guess. The search engine will respond with a "did you mean," "we have included," or similar phrase that will probably show results for the correct spelling of a word.

CHAPTER FIVE

You've Got Mail!

Do you use your computer to send or receive email? This has become one of the most popular uses of the Internet.

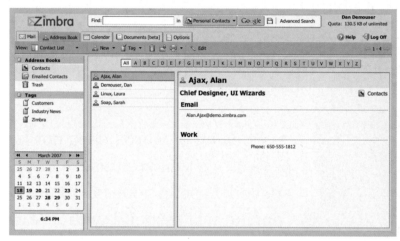

In order to use email (electronic mail), you must have an email address. Many different websites offer email addresses, which usually don't cost anything. If you get one through Google, your email address will be something like yourname@gmail.com. (@ stands for at). If you get your emial address through AOL, it would be something like yourname@aol.com.

Email Facts

- It is estimated that about 200 billion email messages are sent per day. That would be about 2 million emails per second. Of the 200 billion emails sent each day, about 70% are spam or viruses. That means for every 100 emails sent to your email address, 70 are junk emails and only 30 are messages from family and friends.

- About one out of every six people, or 1.2 billion people, worldwide is an email user.

Email User

When you click on your email account by using your Internet browser, you might find new email in your inbox. The email could be a note from a friend, an invitation to a party, or even pictures of your baseball game. Email is also a way to keep in touch with family

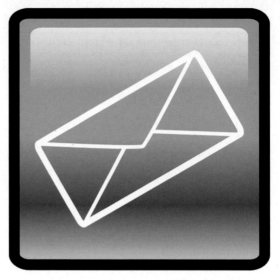

and friends who live in a different city, or even a different country. If your grandparents can't come to your birthday party, wouldn't it be a nice surprise for them to get an email thank-you note from you with pictures of your birthday party attached?

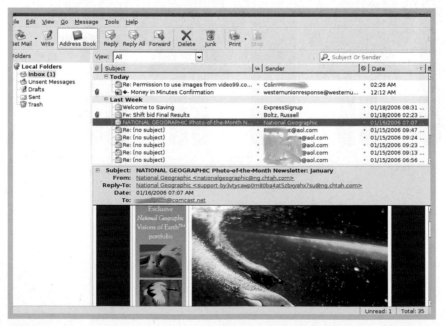

Some people get hundreds of emails every day!

People have gotten so used to the speed of email that they sometimes call regular mail snail mail, because it is so slow to arrive.

Inbox (12)
Starred
Chats
Sent Mail
Drafts
All Mail
Spam (187)
Trash
Contacts

Spam

Have you ever gone to your regular mailbox and found it filled with ads, fliers, and other pieces of mail you were not expecting and which you sometimes toss right into the trash? At times, you might receive more trash than real mail. The same goes for email. People call this spam, which is the email equivalent of what some people call junk mail.

CHAPTER SIX

History of the Internet

Who started the Internet? No one person invented it. It actually began during the 1960s, long before homes had personal computers in them.

The government agency that developed this computer communication system was called the Advanced Research Projects Agency (ARPA). It was part of the government's Department of Defense. What was later known as the Internet had its beginnings in a system called the ARPANET. Like the Internet, it did not need one central location, so if one computer broke down, other computers could still communicate with each other.

Sputnik

Did you know...

Many people think that the Internet was created during the Cold War as a way for the United States Government to protect computer data from a nuclear bomb. But this is not quite true.

Russia became the world leader in technology when they launched the satellite, Sputnik, in 1957. The United States Defense Department responded to Sputnik's launch by creating ARPA in 1958. Then on December 6, 1967, they decided to spend $19,800 for the design and specification of a computer network. The result was a four-month long study that led to the formation of the ARPANET. Without Sputnik, we might not have the Internet today.

CHAPTER SEVEN
Universities and the Net

Because universities have been involved in research for the government, ARPANET also connected computers at universities involved in government research. It was not long before people using these computers began leaving messages for each other. These messages were the earliest versions of what we now call email.

We're so used to instant messaging, text messaging, and chatting online, that it's hard for us to imagine how amazing those first communications over the ARPANET were.

1969

2008

On October, 29, 1969 the first message was sent by Charley Kline, a student at the University of California, Los Angeles, to the Stanford Research Institute. The message was supposed to say "login" but only the "l" and "o" were sent. This means the first email ever sent said "lo".

The first email message was sent in California from UCLA to Stanford University.

University of California, Los Angeles

Stanford University

CHAPTER EIGHT

Personal Computers and the Net

In the mid-1970s, computers started getting small and inexpensive enough for people to have them in their homes.

Many home computer users started using the network to communicate between computers and share messages with each other.

The Language of Computers

You may wonder how computers talk to each other. In 1963, the American Standard Code for Information Interchange (ASCII) was developed. Different manufacturers use the same 128 codes to make the English alphabet, Arabic numerals, punctuation marks, and many other things.

ASCII Alphabet							
A	1	0	0	0	0	0	1
B	1	0	0	0	0	1	0
C	1	0	0	0	0	1	1
D	1	0	0	0	1	0	0
E	1	0	0	0	1	0	1
F	1	0	0	0	1	1	0
G	1	0	0	0	1	1	1
H	1	0	0	1	0	0	0
I	1	0	0	1	0	0	1
J	1	0	0	1	0	1	0
K	1	0	0	1	0	1	1
L	1	0	0	1	1	0	0
M	1	0	0	1	1	0	1
N	1	0	0	1	1	1	0
O	1	0	0	1	1	1	1
P	1	0	1	0	0	0	0
Q	1	0	1	0	0	0	1
R	1	0	1	0	0	1	0
S	1	0	1	0	0	1	1
T	1	0	1	0	1	0	0
U	1	0	1	0	1	0	1
V	1	0	1	0	1	1	0
W	1	0	1	0	1	1	1
X	1	0	1	1	0	0	0
Y	1	0	1	1	0	0	1
Z	1	0	1	1	0	1	0

What you type: h   i   b   y   e

What your computer reads: 1001000   1001001   1000010   1011001   1000101

During the last half of the 1970s, it was obvious that ARPANET wasn't big enough to handle all of this activity. The program was shifted to the National Science Foundation (NSF), which developed a larger network called the NSFNET. In 1990, this became known as the Internet.

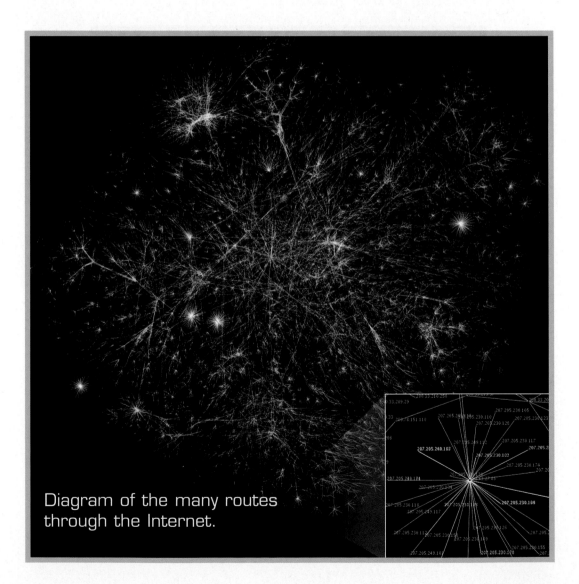

Diagram of the many routes through the Internet.

How Does Email Travel?

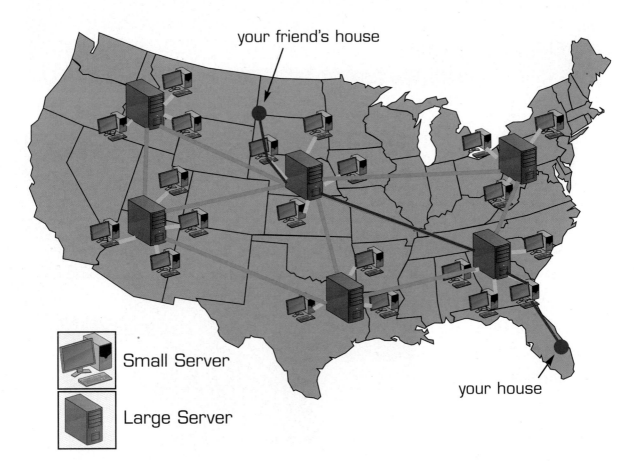

your friend's house

Small Server

Large Server

your house

Email travels along imaginary roads from your computer to one or more servers and then to your friend's computer.

Servers are the key to sending and receiving emails. You can think of servers like bridges. Some bridges are small carrying only a few cars. Other bridges are very large carrying many, many cars. If the bridge goes down, no traffic gets through. It's the same on the Internet, if a server goes down your email can't travel from your computer to your friend's computer.

CHAPTER NINE

The Net Grows and Changes

Though the Internet attracted a lot of email activity, it wasn't until the beginning of the World Wide Web in 1991 that people started to understand and explore just how much they could do with a home computer.

This NeXTcube used by Berners-Lee at CERN became the first Web server.

No one owns or runs the World Wide Web. It is a network of websites that continues to just grow and grow. The idea that people would use the Internet at home to shop,

play games, or read the newspaper was never part of the plan of those who developed the ARPANET. They had no idea how much and how quickly personal computers would change the way we live.

America Online

In 1991, during the early days of the World Wide Web, a company named Quantum Computer Services changed its name to America Online. Many computer users started using the Internet and email for the first time through AOL. The company quickly became the biggest Internet service provider.

AOL.

CHAPTER TEN
Social Networks and Chat Rooms

Some websites serve as places where friends can connect, put up pictures, and keep in touch. These are called social networking sites and have become very popular in recent years.

Two of the most popular sites for teenagers are Facebook (www.facebook.com) and MySpace (www.myspace.com).

Websites officer a couple of different ways for you to communicate online. Two common types of online communication are chat rooms and message boards. In a chat room, you can only communicate with those who have signed up to enter the same room of a specific website.

Message boards usually have a number of responses to a single subject that you can read or contribute to. These allow people to connect with others who have similar interests.

How Do 10-13 Year Olds Use the Internet?

Internet Uses	Percent of U.S. 10-13 Year Olds
Schoolwork	77%
Email	64%
Play games	65%
Listen to the radio or watch movies	18%
Chat rooms	16%

CHAPTER ELEVEN

Play It Safe On the Internet!

The more that you communicate with people over the Internet, the more careful you have to be. Your parents have probably told you never to get into a car with a stranger. You must be just as careful on the Internet.

On the Internet, you should never reveal personal information like your age or where you live to people you do not know. Because you can't see them over the Internet, people can pretend to be someone they are not. The person who says she is a 12-year-old girl could even be a 50-year-old man!

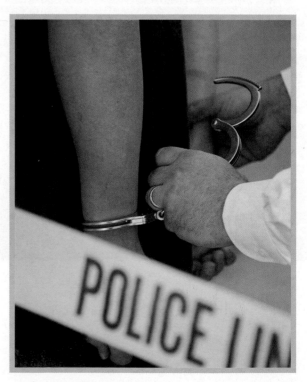

People who use the Internet to pretend to be someone they are not may be arrested and charged as an Internet predator.

You should never agree to meet in person someone you have only met over the Internet. It is important to act responsibly when you are online. In order to be safe, always ask an adult if you have any questions about people you meet online or about different websites.

CHAPTER TWELVE
Attachments and Viruses

Sometimes we send or receive files with lots of information on them as an email attachment. This attachment might have a lot of words in it or it might be a photo attachment.

You open an attachment by double clicking where it says attachment or has an icon such as a paper clip. Opening and saving an attachment on your computer is called downloading. You should never download an attachment without checking with an adult.

Sometimes attachments come with viruses in them. In the world of medicine, a virus is something that gets into your body and makes you sick. In the computer world, a virus can make your computer sick! It can erase files that are stored in your computer or even make your computer stop working! You should be very careful about downloading an attachment that might be carrying a virus. There are antivirus programs you can purchase and download into your computer that will check for viruses automatically.

CHAPTER THIRTEEN

Cyberspace Continues to Expand

Today, it is common for people to watch TV programs on the Internet, listen to music over the Internet, and even make telephone calls using the

Internet. Twenty years ago, we could not imagine how much we would come to rely on our computers. It is just as hard today to imagine how much more the Internet will have to offer us 20 years from now!

You may be able to use your computer with a free Internet phone service, such as Skype. If your computer has a camera you may be able to see your friends and family while you are talking to them.

Today you can download movies and television programs and then watch them on your computer or television. You can choose to buy individual shows and movies or you can buy a subscription plan.

Timeline

 1967: The Defense Department spends $19,800 to study the design and specification of a computer network.

 1968: The study results in the start of the ARPANET, a computer network for the government.

1969: Some universities doing research for the government also started using the ARPANET.

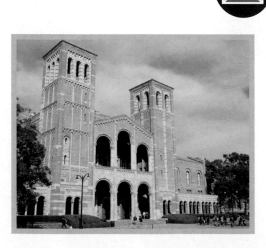

1990: What had been the ARPANET turned into a larger network called the NSFNET. It is known as the Internet, which lots of people can use.

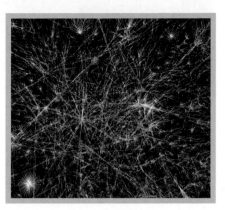

1991: The World Wide Web begins and AOL becomes the most popular service connecting computers to the Internet.

1995: Yahoo.com becomes the first popular website to let people search the web.

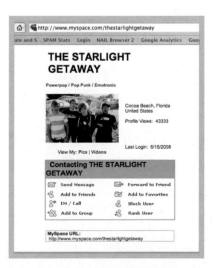

2002: MySpace becomes a popular website for social networking, followed by Facebook in 2003.

Glossary

attachment (uh-TACH-ment): a file that is sent along with an email

chat room (CHAT room): an imaginary room where people who have signed on to enter it can communicate with each other

cyberspace (SY-bur-spayss): the electronic world of computer networks, the invisible space where the Internet exists, and computers communicate with each other

domain (doe-MANE): a website's name

downloading (DOWN-lohd-ing): saving an email attachment or a file to your computer

email (EE-mayl): short for electronic mail, sent over the Internet by one computer user to another

icon (EYE-kon): a picture on your screen that you can click on to open a computer program or file

ISP (EYE-ESS-PEE): Internet Service Provider, the company that you pay each month to connect you to the Internet

message board (MESS-ij BORD): the part of a website that allows people to write comments or exchange messages about a subject

modem (MOH-dum): the part of a computer that provides an online connection

network (NET-wurk): a group of things that are connected to each other

online (ON-LINE): being connected to the Internet, the World Wide Web, or a website

spam (SPAM): email that is sent to thousands or millions of addresses without anyone asking for it

URL (YU-ARE-EL): a Uniform Resource Locator or web address such as www.google.com

virus (VY-russ): something in a computer file or attachment that can make your computer, or certain programs on it, stop working

website (WEB-site): a central location for related web pages on the Internet, like www.facebook.com

Index

Further reading

Oxdale, Chris. *My First Internet Guide*. Heinemann, 2007.
Roddel, Victoria. *Internet Safety Kids' Guide*. Lulu.com, 2007.
Willard, Nancy E. *Cyber-Safe Kids, Cyber-Savvy Teens*. Jossey-Bass, 2007.

Websites

www.fcc.gov/omd/history/internet/
www.internet101.org/
www.familyinternet.about.com/

About the Author

Don McLeese is a journalism professor at the University of Iowa. He has written many articles for newspapers and magazines and many books for young students as well.